GYMNASTICS
UNEVEN BARS

Tips, Rules, and
Legendary Stars

by Tracy Nelson Maurer

Consultant:
Paige Roth
Region IV Xcel Chair
USA Gymnastics Women's Program
Owner, Iowa Gym-Nest

CAPSTONE PRESS
a capstone imprint

Snap Books are published by Capstone Press,
1710 Roe Crest Drive, North Mankato, Minnesota 56003
www.mycapstone.com

Library of Congress Cataloging-in-Publication Data
Names: Maurer, Tracy, 1965- author.
Title: Uneven bars : tips, rules, and legendary stars / by Tracy Nelson Maurer
Description: North Mankato, Minnesota : Capstone Press, 2017. | Series:
   Snap books. Gymnastics | Includes bibliographical references and index.
Identifiers: LCCN 2016002040| ISBN 9781515722199 (library binding) |
   ISBN 9781515722250 (ebook (pdf))
Subjects: LCSH: Uneven parallel bars—Juvenile literature.
Classification: LCC GV536 .M38 2017 | DDC 796.44/2—dc23
LC record available at http://lccn.loc.gov/2016002040

Editorial Credits
Gena Chester, editor
Bobbie Nuytten, designer
Kelly Garvin, media researcher
Tori Abraham, production specialist

Image Credits
Capstone Press, Karon Dubke, 6, 7, 11, 12, 13, 14, 15, 19, 23, 25 (top),
Martin Bustamante, 15, 17; Dreamstime/Ukrphoto, 5, 16; Getty Images,
John Dominis/The LIFE Picture Collection, 26, Pascal Rondeau/Allsport, 28;
Glow/Peter Muller, cover, 8; Newscom: Geoff Burke/USA Today Sports, 24,
Keystone Pictures USA/Zuma Press, 27, Tom Fox/MCT, 29; Shutterstock:
Alex Emanuel Koch, 10, Aspen Photo, 1, Brendan Howard, 21, Fotos593, 25
(bottom), ID1974, 22, prapass, 23, Volt Collection, 9

Artistic Elements: Shutterstock: alexdndz, Bojanovic, Hakki Arslan

Special Thank You
Thank you to the coaches and gymnasts at GK Gymnastics.

Printed in the United States of America in North Mankato, Minnesota.
009686F16

Table of Contents

Take a Swing
on the Uneven Bars

Imagine springing up to the lower uneven bar and holding it for a beat. You release and let your momentum swing you into the next move. You fly fluidly between the lower and upper bar with airborne tricks. One final flip, and you stick your landing.

Routines on the uneven bar **apparatus** are thrilling to watch. They show a gymnast's strength, endurance, and flair. Each routine features moves that flow from one to the next. The entire performance lasts only about 45 seconds. But it takes months and even years of hard practice to polish every detail.

Only women gymnasts compete on the uneven bars and balance beam. Men compete on the parallel bars, the horizontal bar, pommel horse, and rings. All gymnasts compete in the vault and floor exercise events. These events are all part of artistic gymnastics.

Fast Fact:
Artistic gymnastics appeared in the first Olympic Games in 1896 in Athens. Men's rope climbing, parallel bars, and horizontal bar were some of the artistic gymnastics events in 1896.

apparatus—equipment used in gymnastics, such as the uneven bars

CHAPTER 1

Get Fit,
Get Ready

Gymnastics clubs are the easiest, safest, and most efficient way to learn the sport. Your best bet is to join one affiliated with USA Gymnastics. The organization sets rules and standards for clubs and competitions. Go to USA Gymnastics' official website for a list of member clubs near you.

Before you first grip the uneven bars, you need to work out and work hard. Coaches help gymnasts build physical fitness for strength and body control. A gymnast on the uneven bars must be able to hold her own body weight. Chin-ups, pull-ups, and push-ups are common exercises—and that's just for starters! Conditioning at practices may also include core exercises, such as sit ups, planks, and leg lifts. **Aerobic exercises**, such as jumping jacks, are essential for building strength and **stamina**. Muscle stretches occur before and after practices to build flexibility and grace.

Exercising outside of the gym is time well spent. Practice handstands and do sit ups at home. They can help build the balance and strength necessary for skills attempted in the gym. But save your actual uneven bar tricks for the gym. There a **spotter** can make sure you're performing moves correctly and safely.

aerobic exercise—activity that works the heart and lungs
stamina—the energy and strength to keep doing something for a long period of time
spotter—a person who keeps watch to help prevent injury

Changing Apparatus

Uneven bar gymnasts learn basic skills on a single, low bar. They add the second bar as they build skills and gain confidence.

The bar height can be adjusted for all but the top competitors. Beginners should use a bar set at chest height. Advanced gymnasts must use the apparatus with the lower bar 5.5 feet (1.7 meters) above the floor. The upper bar must stand at 8.2 feet (2.5 m) or higher from the floor.

The distance between the bars gives gymnasts room to perform tricks. In the early days of the event, the bars were set about shoulder-width apart. Routines then focused on swinging moves, simple rotations around the bars, and handstands or holds. As gymnasts added more difficult tricks, they needed more space between the bars. Today the two bars are spread about 6 feet (1.8 m) apart.

Fast Fact:
Uneven bars first appeared at an international competition in 1934 at the Artistic Gymnastics World Championships in Budapest. This was also the first women's World Championships.

Better Bars

Until the 1960s, uneven bars were oval shaped and made of wood. They sometimes broke during routines. Today bars are made of **fiberglass** with wood around it. Bars are round so they're easier to grip. Anchor cables also make the apparatus safer by providing extra support.

Safety First!

Falls are common, especially as you learn new moves on the uneven bars. Mats on the floor cushion falls. Injuries can be avoided by falling safely. Land on the mat with your arms tucked in, never outstretched or reaching behind your body. Always work out on the uneven bars with a spotter near the apparatus ready to help you.

fiberglass—a strong, lightweight material made from thin threads of glass

Practice and Performance Gear

Gymnasts come to the gym ready to train. They wear stretchy, close-fitting clothing to prevent fabric from wrapping around the bars and causing accidents.

At competitions gymnasts wear **leotards**. Team members must wear matching leotards. They wear tracksuits before and after performing to keep their muscles warm.

Many gymnasts wear braces called grips on both hands to help prevent painful blisters from forming when their palms rub against the bar. Grips help keep their hands from slipping off the bar too.

Each grip has a leather strip from the wrist to the fingertips. The middle and fourth fingertips slip into two holes in the strip. The grip wraps tightly at the wrist. Chalk is added to hands and the grips to absorb sweat. Most gymnasts also wear wristbands under the grip to limit sweat. A small wooden dowel under the leather at their fingertips can be added for extra gripping power.

leotard—a snug, one-piece garment worn by gymnasts and dancers

CHAPTER 2

Get a
Grip

Working the uneven bars requires a strong grip. But not just any grip! Every move uses a certain grip position. Grips can either provide stability or add difficulty to a move. They help the routine flow smoothly from trick to trick.

Judges at competitions check grip positions. They also look for powerful releases. A release is when a gymnast lets go of the bar for a trick and then grabs it again.

Grip Positions

Over or Regular Grip

Knuckles face up, palms face away

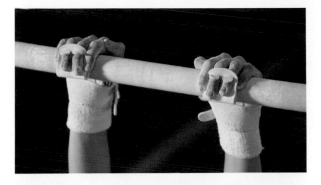

Under or Reverse Grip

Knuckles face away, palms face you

Mixed Grip

One over and one under grip

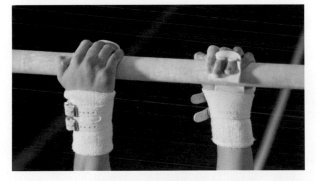

Eagle, L, or Dorsal Grip

Arms rotated with elbows facing forward, hands in an over grip with thumbs pointed away from the body

Each bar routine has three phases: the **mount** onto the bars, a series of skills, and the **dismount**. Judges score every element of each phase.

Phase 1: The Mount

The mount sets the routine in motion. Beginning gymnasts can simply hop up and grab the low bar. Part of the mount is getting into position for the first element. A gymnast may start by pulling the body up and over the bar for a pullover. They might also start by hanging in basic positions, such as a pike, straddle, or tuck.

Gymnasts add difficulty to the mount with a kip, which is a move that helps a gymnast gain momentum. Remember pumping a swing at the playground to fly higher? The glide kip works somewhat like that. It helps position the body for the next skill and connects skills together.

Advanced gymnasts may choose to use a **springboard** to **somersault** or twist onto the bars. Some athletes leapfrog the low bar to reach the high bar!

a pullover

mount—a move done to get on an apparatus
dismount—a move done to get off of an apparatus
springboard—a strong, flexible board that is used for jumping very high
somersault—a gymnastics move where you tuck your head into your chest and roll in a circle

Basic Hangs

Shoulders stay below the bar and arms hang straight from the bar.

Pike
Bend at the hips, legs stretched out straight

Tuck
Tuck both legs up to the chest

Straddle
Make a "V" with straight legs

The Glide Kip

1. From the floor or a springboard, jump with your arms reaching for the low bar. Use an over grip to hang from the bar as your body glides and extends under the bar with your legs straight in a pike or straddle position.

2. Lift your toes up to the bar and swing back.

3. Use the swing's energy to pull your body up as you push down on the bar. Keep your arms straight. Bring your hips to the bar into a front support. Look straight ahead.

Phase 2: The Routine

This is where the high-flying action takes off! Gymnasts push the difficulty levels of skills with awesome results.

Elite gymnasts compete using rules set by the Fédération Internationale de Gymnastique (FIG). The rules are listed in the official rule book called the Code of Points. Junior Olympic athletes at the lower levels use the USA Gymnastics Junior Olympic Code of Points. The required elements in an elite routine come from five groups:

1. casts, which look like a power pump for momentum
2. forward and backward giant swings that make a complete rotation around the bar and end in a handstand
3. circle swings, including hips and shoulders swinging around the bar in a pike or straddle from one handstand into another
4. release moves
5. dismounts

elite—describes gymnasts who are among the best

The Back Hip Circle

Remember to keep your arms straight.

1. First do a cast, a pump for momentum to launch the rotation. Move your legs forward then backward and up as you push down on the bar.

2. Bring your hips back to the bar. Lean your shoulders back as your legs move forward under the bar.

3. Angle your legs about 45 degrees and spin around the bar in a full circle.

Fast Fact:
If a gymnast falls in competition, she can immediately return to the bars and continue the routine.

Phase 3: The Dismount

The last phase of a routine is often the most suspenseful to watch. Excitement in the audience reaches its peak when a gymnast lands her dismount perfectly.

Beginning gymnasts release the bar and add flair to their landing with an underswing or a sole circle. Advanced gymnasts spin, flip, or twist in daring moves down from the bars.

The triple back tuck, or Magaña, ranks as one of the most difficult dismounts. It requires three tucked rotations from the high bar. It's rarely attempted in competitions.

All gymnasts try to stick their landing. Wobbles or steps backward or forward lower the score. According to the FIG Code of Points, failure to land feet first is a minimum 1.00 point deduction.

Fast Fact:
Brenda Magaña Almaral of Mexico was the first to land the triple back tuck in 2002.

CHAPTER 3

Meet to Compete

Practices, workouts, bruises, and sore muscles all come together in less than a minute at a competition, or meet. Members of USA Gymnastics can compete in meets at the local, state, and national levels.

USA Gymnastics uses 10 levels for developing gymnasts. Gymnasts must master a certain set of skills before moving up to the next level. The highest level in USA Gymnastics is Elite. Gymnasts who are not at Elite can compete as Junior Olympic gymnasts.

For the uneven bar, everyone in Levels 1 through 5 performs a **compulsory** routine. Routines are specific to each level. Gymnasts work on just the lower bar until Level 4. Level 5 works with two bars but is still required to do a compulsory routine. In Levels 6 through Elite, gymnasts create their own routines with the required elements on both bars.

Junior Elites are ages 11 to 15. Senior Elites are at least 16 years old. The top competitors for each elite division may be selected to join the U.S. National Team. The U.S. Olympic committee chooses a team of five to eight Senior Elite members from the National Team. The decision is based mostly on the gymnasts' performances at the Olympic Trials.

Other countries use different systems. For example, Canada has four main divisions. From lowest to highest, the divisions are Aspire, High Performance, Canadian JO Program, and Nation. Each division has subdivisions with varying levels of skill.

Fast Fact:
Gymnasts in elite divisions usually train from 30 to 40 hours a week.

compulsory—a required element or routine

Excellent Options

USA Gymnastics offers another competitive program called Xcel. The program is for gymnasts who love the sport but can't train as much as Junior Olympic gymnasts. Typically gymnasts are required to practice a minimum of 4 hours per week to compete in the beginning Xcel division.

an artistic gymnastics competition in Moscow, Russia

A major gymnastics competition fills an arena with families, friends, and fans. Vault, uneven bars, balance beam, and floor exercises often happen at the same time in the same gymnasium. Music from the floor exercise blares over cheers for uneven bar tricks. The atmosphere is noisy and exciting.

Each event has compulsory skills that show gymnasts' abilities, creativity, and style. These skills are combined to form elements to make up a routine. Depending on the competition, two to eight judges evaluate each routine. Elite gymnasts hope for high 15s and 16s. But it's possible to score above 17. The maximum Junior Olympic and Xcel score is 10 points.

Individual gymnasts can win medals in a single event, such as the uneven bars, or for all-around. The best scores combined from all of the events determine all-around medals. Gymnasts can also win medals as a team.

Difficulty - D Score

Every element in a routine is separated and scored. It is then assigned a point value based on difficulty. The easiest element, or A, has a value of 0.1. Difficulty increases with each letter. After A, the next highest difficulty is B. For each additional letter there is an increase of 0.1 in points. Judges also give "connection" points for linking the top elements in a performance. The gymnast receives 0.50 points for each completed requirement as well.

Execution - E Score

Each judge starts at 10. They subtract 0.1 for tiny mistakes and up to a whole point for large mistakes, such as a fall. The highest and lowest scores from the judges are tossed out. The average of the remaining scores is the E score. Once both the D and F scores are determined, they are added together for one final score.

Fast Fact:
Four gymnasts tied for Gold in the uneven bars at the 2015 World Championships. The four-way tie was a historic first for the Championships. Viktoria Komova and Daria Spiridonova of Russia earned a winning score of 15.366. Fan Yilin of China and Madison Kocian of the United States scored the exact same number to win as well.

Gymnasts want to look strong and confident performing their tricks on the uneven bars. They also want to emphasize their unique style through their appearance.

Hairstyles must keep hair from the face. Gymnasts might have short haircuts with high bangs or long hair pulled up with a few small braids in a bun, ponytail, or pigtails. Most gymnasts match their leotards to their hair ties. Bobby pins, butterfly clips, and loads of gel and hairspray keep hair-dos in place.

Some older gymnasts add to their look with makeup. Brazilian gymnast Daniele Hypolito wore vibrant green, yellow, and blue eye shadow at the 2012 Olympics. Many gymnasts wear eyeliner and waterproof mascara. A few wear glitter around their eyes or in their hair. Some wear bold lip stain for color. Others go for a more natural look with neutral colors and clear lip gloss.

Daniele Hypolito's eye shadow matched Brazil's national colors.

Your Gym Bag Packing List

Pack your bag the night before a competition. This will save you time and stress on the day you compete.

- water bottle
- towel
- hand grips
- chalk powder
- makeup
- hairbrush, clips, ties, and hair products
- gym slippers if you don't perform in bare feet

CHAPTER 4

Legends of the
Uneven Bars

From attempting the hardest moves to inventing new ones, some athletes have left a lasting impression on the uneven bars event. Their athleticism and grace has influenced the way we see gymnastics today. And their stories of success inspire young gymnasts around the world.

Olga Korbut

Olga Korbut shook up the gymnastics world in 1972 during the Olympic events. At 17 years old, Olga competed in the balance beam, floor, and uneven bars events as the youngest person on the team for the Soviet Union. She won three gold medals and one silver medal.

During the uneven bars event, Olga performed an aerial backward somersault from a standing position on the high bar. She was the first gymnast ever to perform this move at the Olympics. It was later named the Korbut Flip in the FIG Code of Points. During the routine, she also nailed a back flip from the low bar to the high bar. The audience loved it! When the judges gave her only a 9.8 out of 10 points, fans yelled and stomped their feet. Today moves from the feet, such as the Korbut Flip, are banned from competition.

Nadia Comaneci

At 14 years old, Nadia Comaneci represented Romania in the uneven bars event at the 1976 Olympic Games. She was the first Olympic gymnast to receive a perfect score, which was 10 points then. But the scoreboard wasn't designed to show 10. Her score came up as 1.0. It confused the crowd at first.

Nadia earned seven perfect scores at the 1976 Games, winning three gold medals for the uneven bars, balance beam, and individual all-around. She also won a bronze medal and a team silver medal. Nadia won two more gold and silver medals at the 1980 Olympic Games.

The Comaneci Salto

The Comaneci Salto is a move named after gymnast Nadia Comaneci. It starts from a front support. The gymnast casts and pushes away from the bar. Then she flips forward for the Salto in a straddle position and catches the bar in a hang.

Fast Fact:
When a gymnast invents a new skill, it must be performed at a World Gymnastics Championship or Olympics competition to be named for her in the FIG Code of Points.

Shannon Miller

As a baby, Shannon Miller wore a brace attached to her feet to keep her legs from growing inward. She overcame this first challenge with the same determination that helped her become an elite gymnast. In the 1992 Olympics Games, she represented the United States in the balance beam, floor exercise, and uneven bars events. Shannon was the first American to win five gold medals in any sport at the Olympic Games.

Shannon competed in 1996 with the "Magnificent Seven" Olympic team that earned the U.S. gymnastics team its first team gold medal. She has seven Olympic medals and nine World Championship medals. She's the only woman in any sport to be inducted into the United States Olympic Hall of Fame twice, as an individual and as a team.

Fast Fact:
The Code of Points includes two skills with Shannon's name on them. The Miller features a cast to a handstand, followed by a one-and-a-half turn to a mixed-L grip on the uneven bars.

Nastia Liukin

Nastia Liukin won the World Gymnastics title in 2005 on the uneven bars. At the 2008 Olympics, Nastia performed an Ono **pirouette** on the high bar. She followed it with a full-twisting pirouette on one hand and a half-turn. The increase in difficulty level set her apart from the rest of the competitors, and she became the individual all-around champion.

During the 2008 Olympics, she was also part of a scoring oddity. She was tied with Chinese gymnast He Kexin at 16.725 after her brilliant routine on the uneven bars. But Olympic rules after 1996 allowed no ties. Instead the winner is determined by the lowest average of deductions. Nastia lost by 0.033.

pirouette—a ballet move where the dancer spins to complete a full circle

As with other sports, there are no shortcuts to success in gymnastics. Winning a 45-second uneven bars routine takes a great deal of practice. But it's easy to find gymnasts around the world who are willing to give it their all for the sport.

GLOSSARY

aerobic exercise (air-OH-bik EK-sur-size)—activity that works the heart and lungs

apparatus (a-puh-RA-tuhs)—equipment used in gymnastics, such as the uneven bars

compulsory (kuhm-PUHL-sur-ee)—a required element or routine

dismount (diss-MOUNT)—a move done to get off of an apparatus

elite (i-LEET)—describes gymnasts who are among the best

fiberglass (FY-buhr-glas)—a strong, lightweight material made from thin threads of glass

leotard (LEE-uh-tard)—a snug, one-piece garment worn by gymnasts and dancers

mount (MOWNT)—a move done to get on an apparatus

pirouette (peer-OOH-et)—a ballet move where the dancer spins to complete a full circle

spotter (SPOT-uhr)—a person who keeps watch to help prevent injury

springboard (SPRING-bord)—a strong, flexible board that is used for jumping very high

somersault (SUHM-ur-sawlt)—a gymnastics move where you tuck your head into your chest and roll in a circle

stamina (STAM-uh-nuh)—the energy and strength to keep doing something for a long period of time

READ MORE

Carmichael, L.E. *The Science Behind Gymnastics*. Science of the Summer Olympics. North Mankato: Capstone Press, 2016.

Savage, Jeff. *Top 25 Gymnastics Skills, Tips, and Tricks*. Berkeley Heights, N.J.: Enslow Publishers, Inc., 2012.

Schlegel, Elfi. *The Gymnastics Book: The Young Performer's Guide to Gymnastics*. 2nd Ed. Buffalo, N.Y.: Firefly Books, 2012.

INTERNET SITES

FactHound offers a safe, fun way to find Internet sites related to this book. All of the sites on FactHound have been researched by our staff.

Here's all you do:

Visit *www.facthound.com*

Type in this code: 9781515722199

Super-cool stuff! Check out projects, games and lots more at
www.capstonekids.com

INDEX